Vol 5

MAZE

Ages 4-6

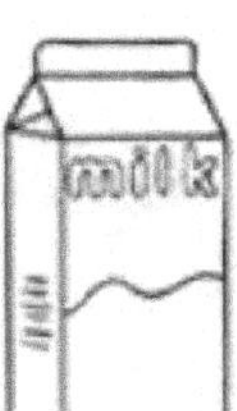

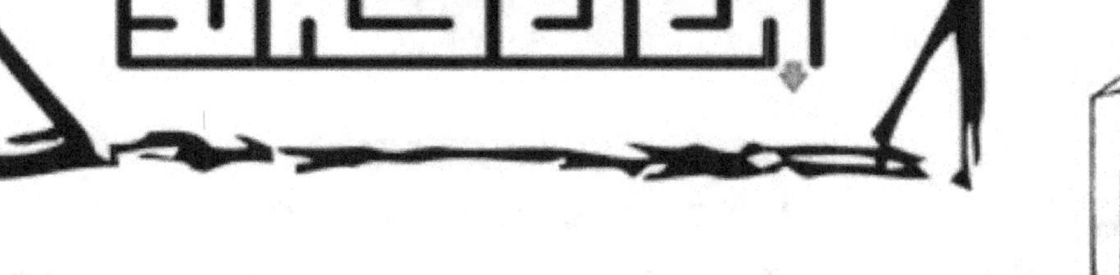

MAZE BOOK

SOCIAL MEDIA

f /MySweetBooks1

t /MySweetBooks1

ig /MySweetBooks1

p /MySweetBooks

Email Us : mysweetbooks1@gmail.com

Milk

MILK

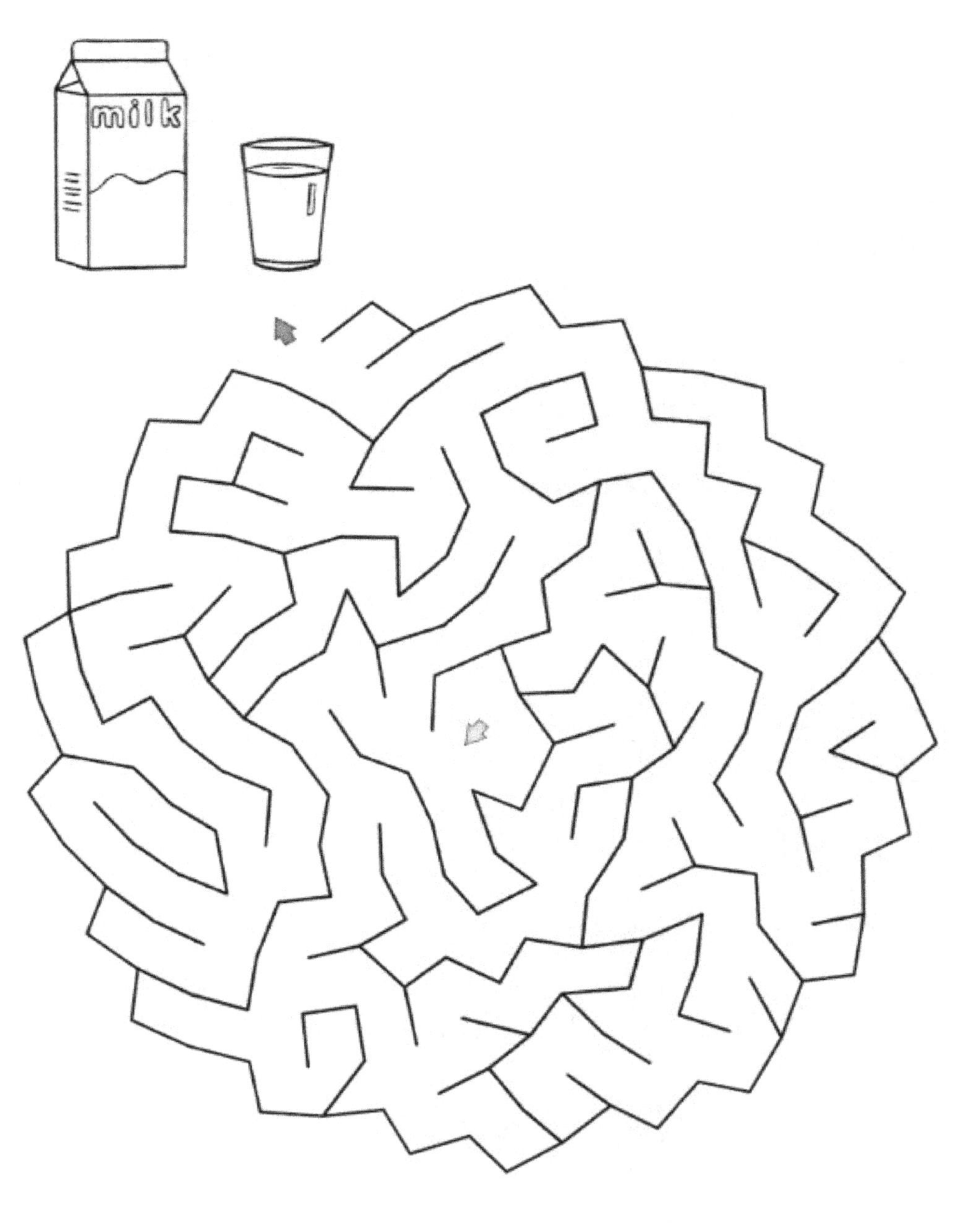

Milk

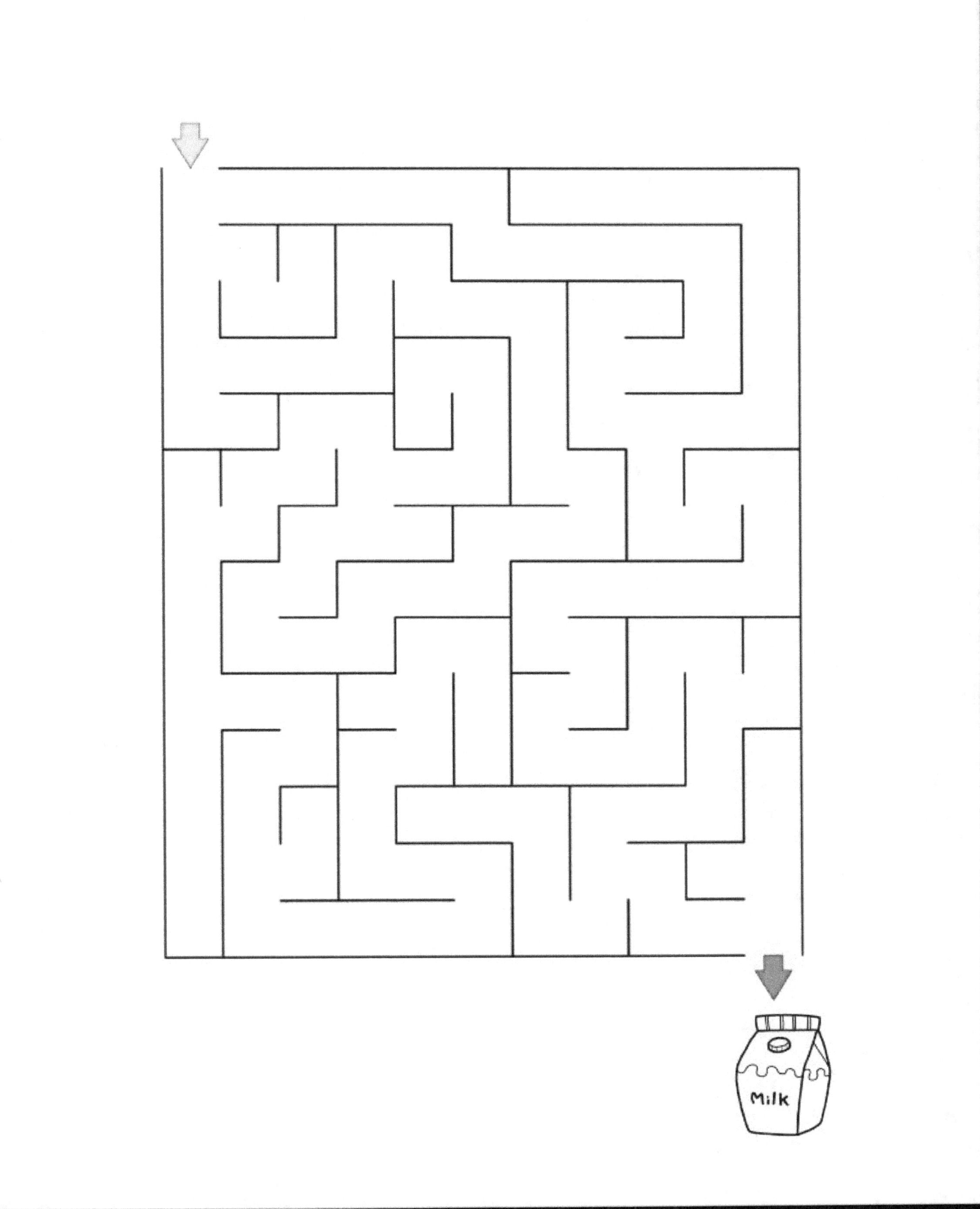
Milk

MILK

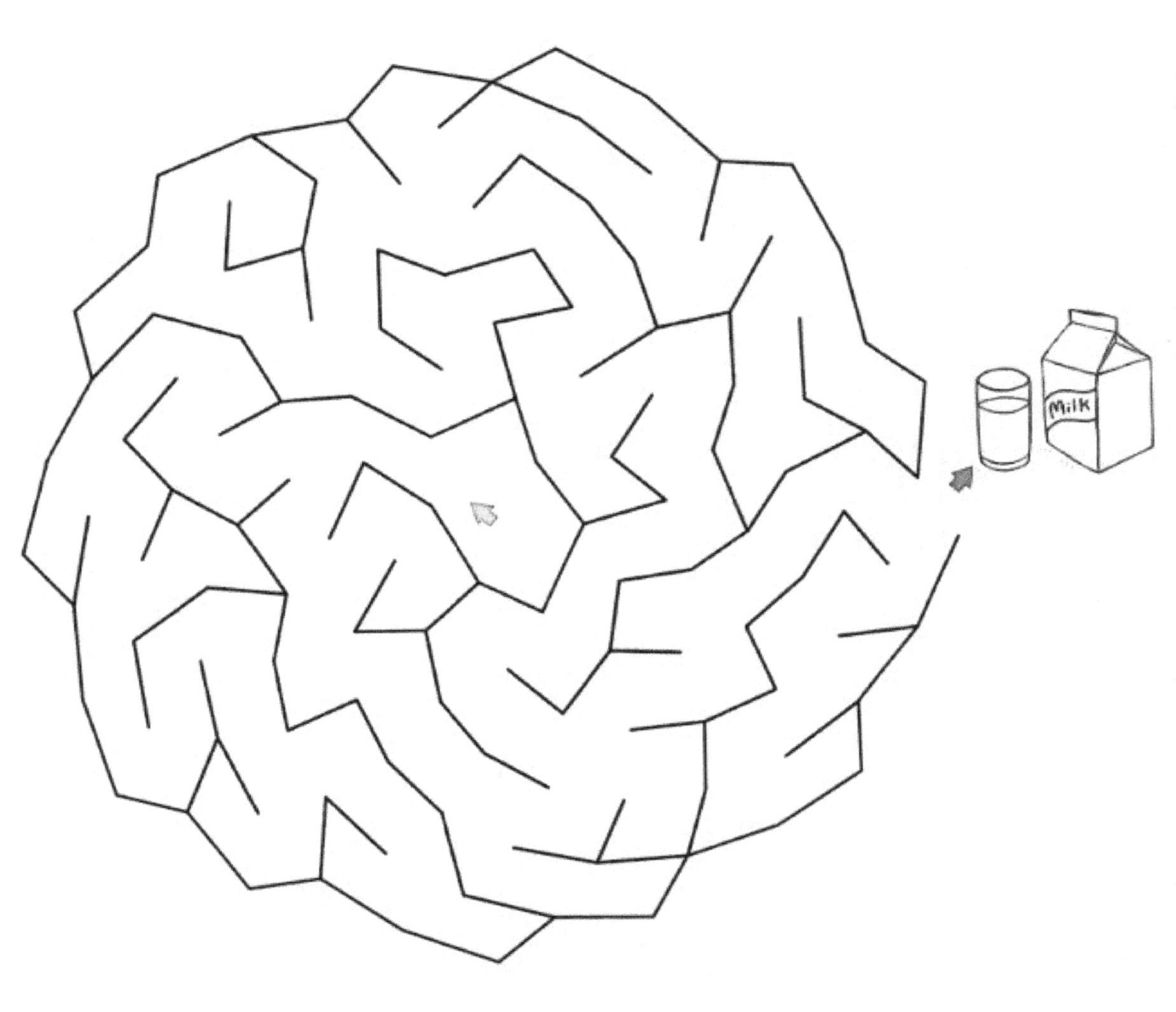

Milk

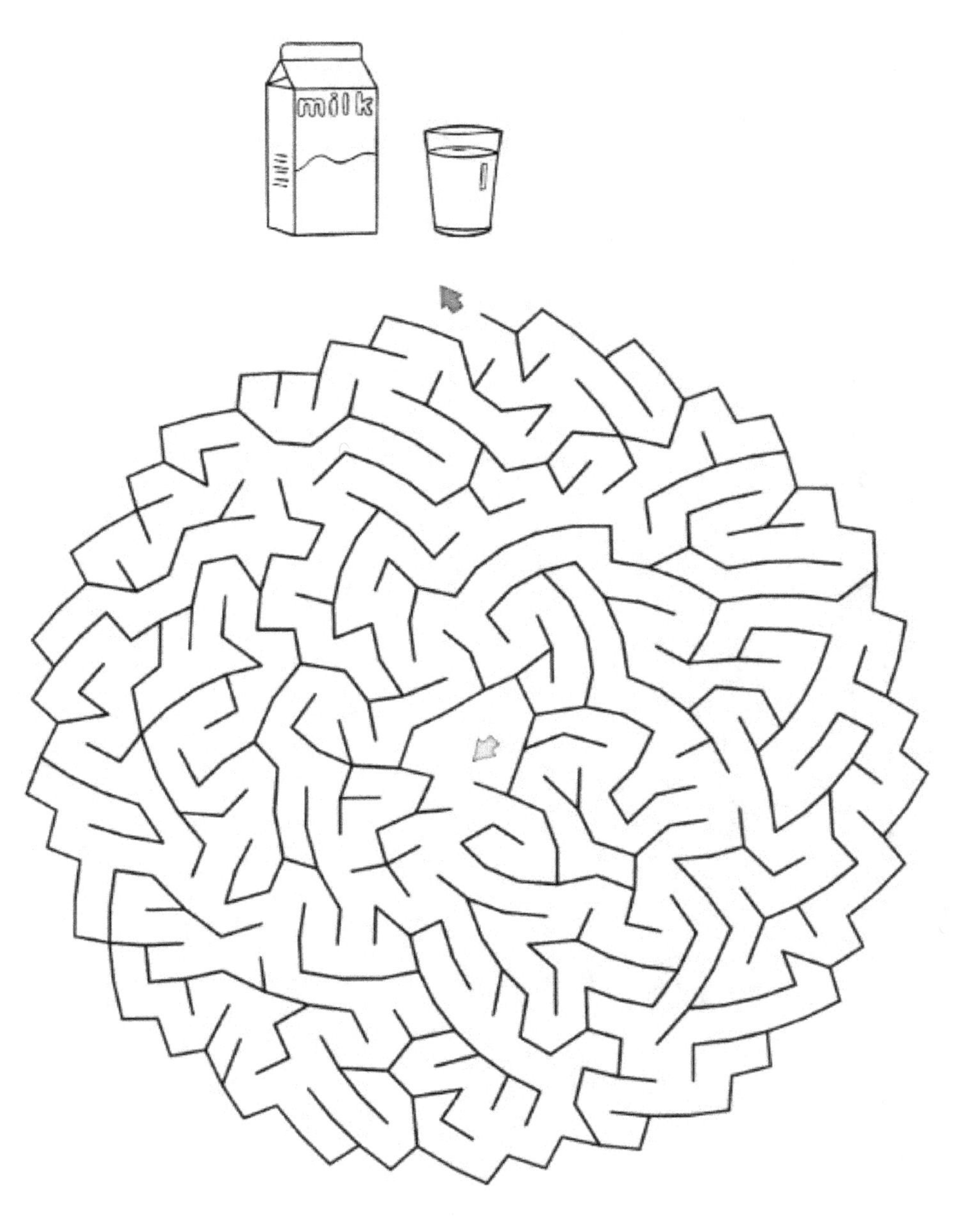

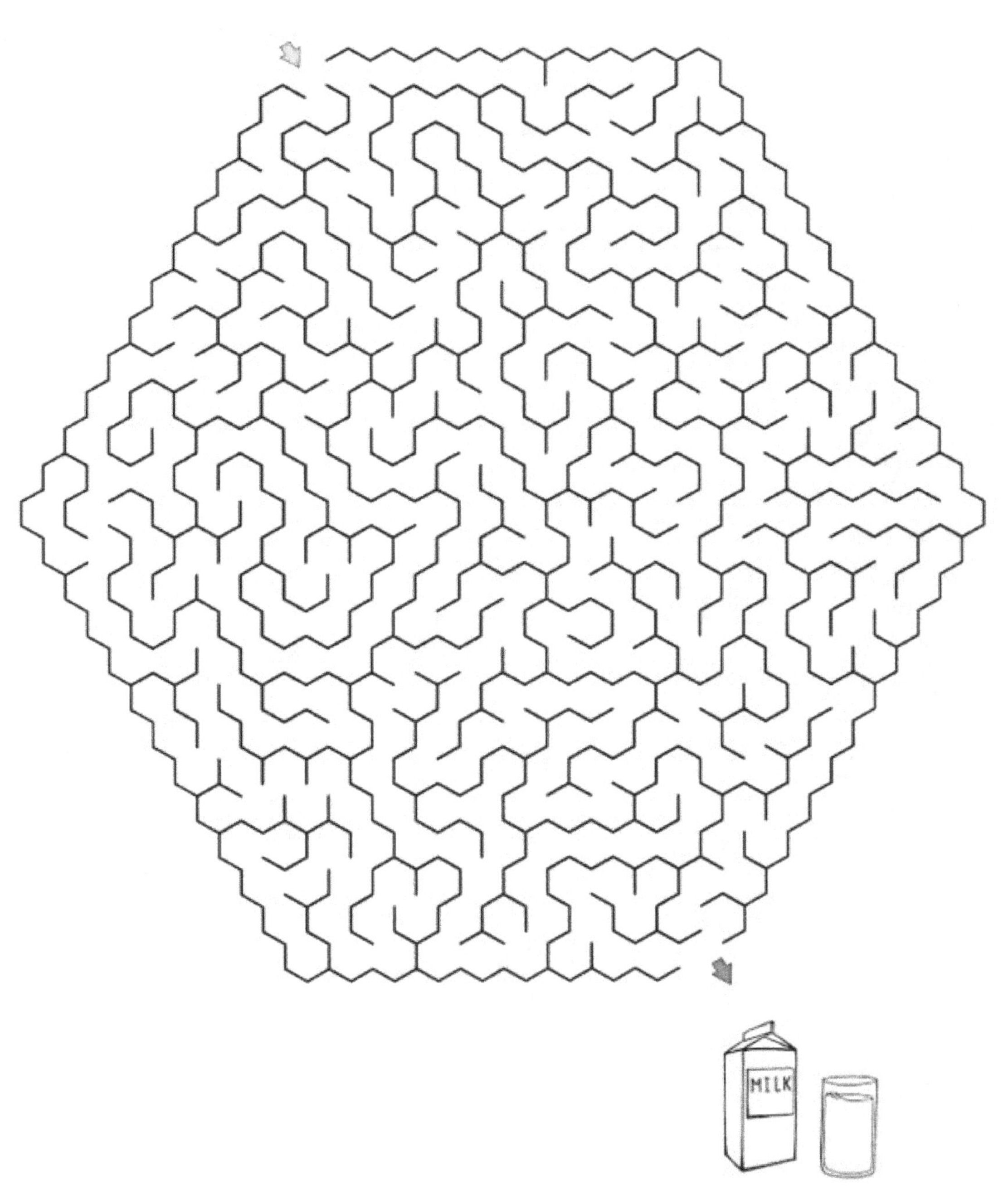
MILK

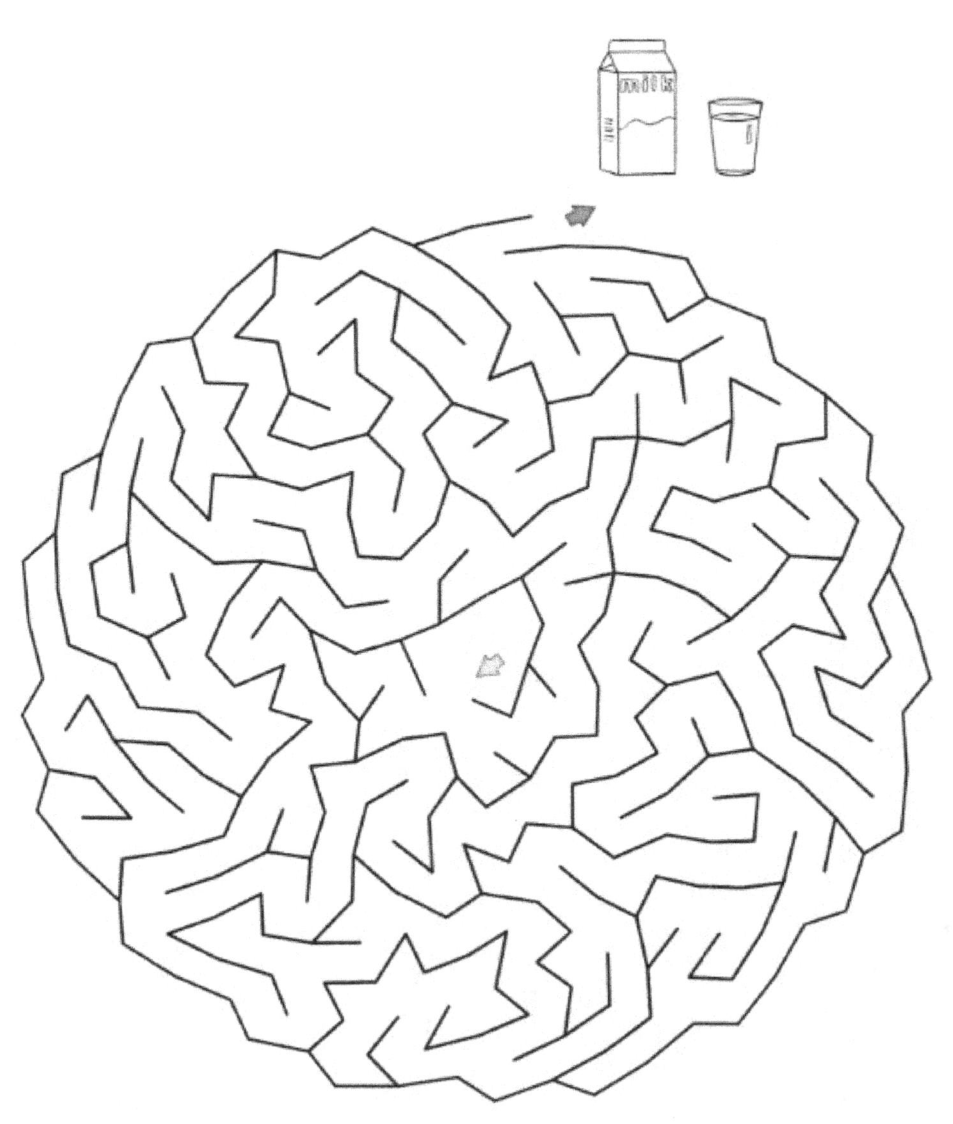

milk

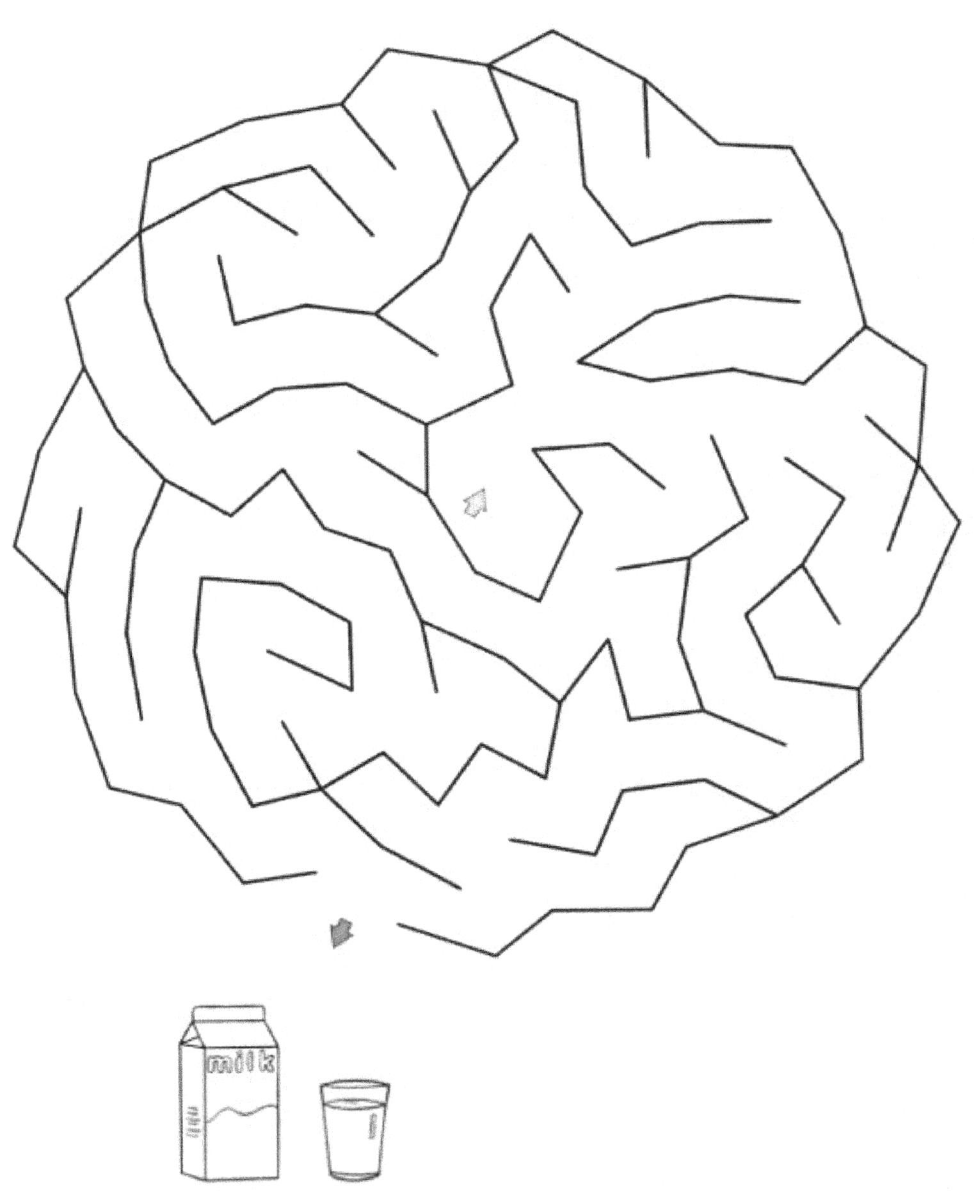

MILK

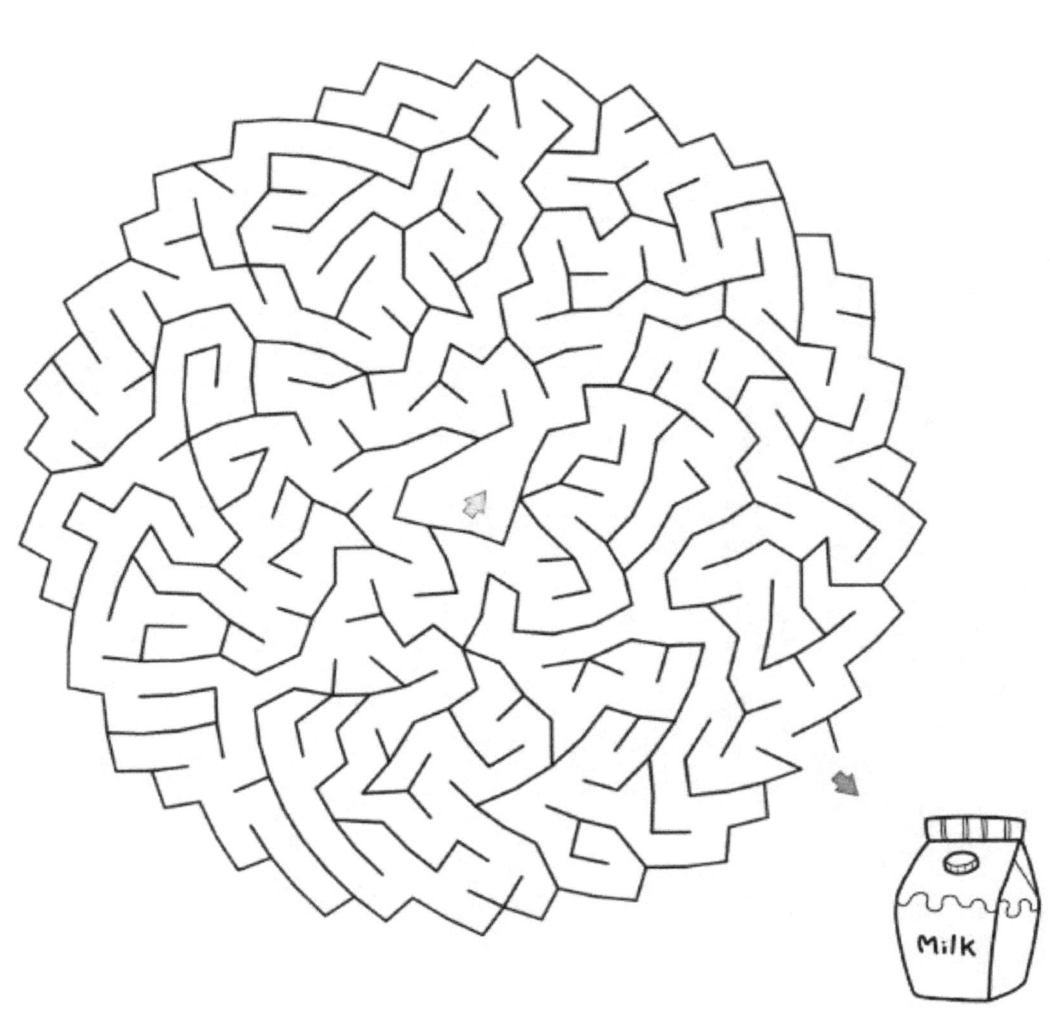

Milk

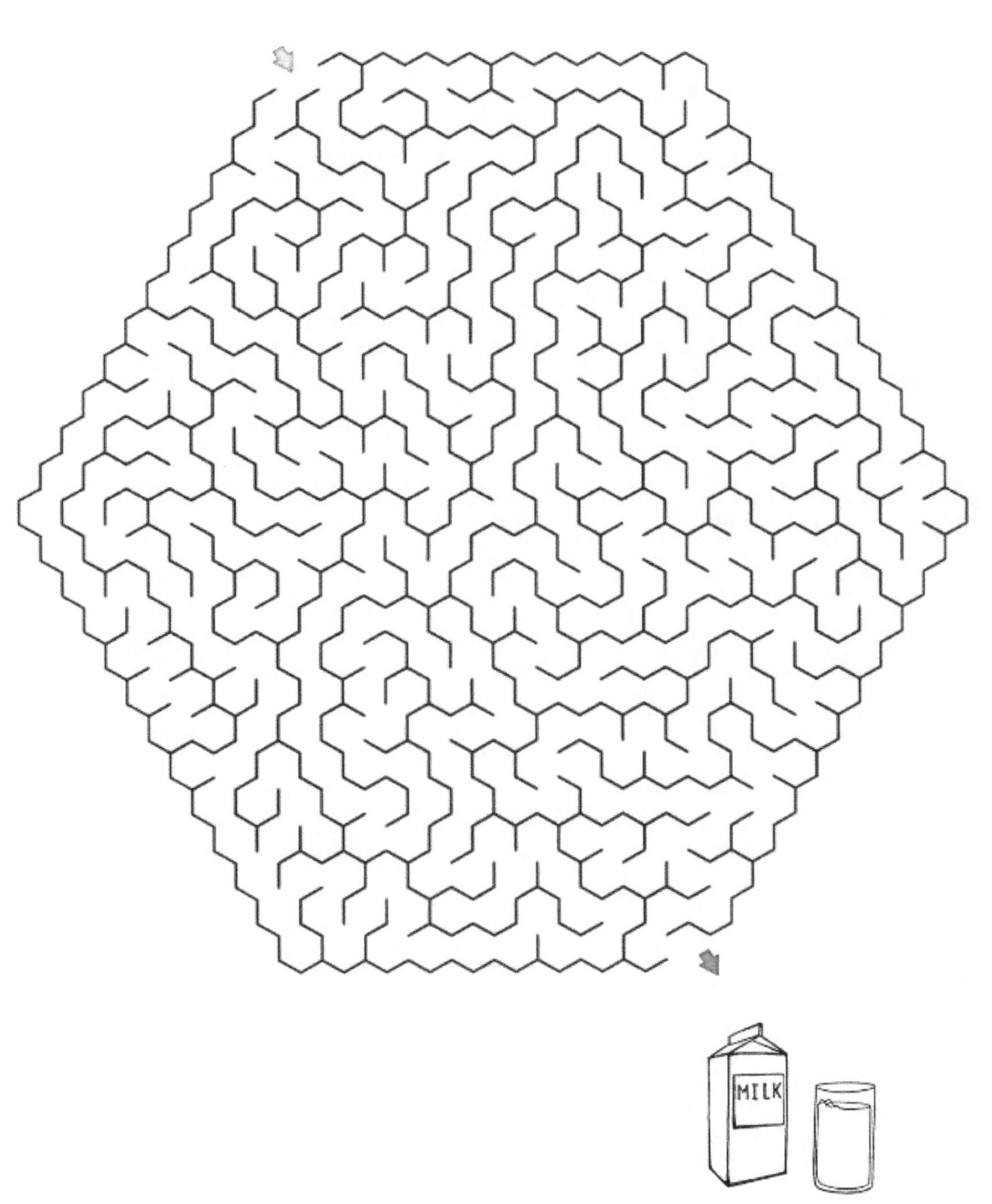

milk

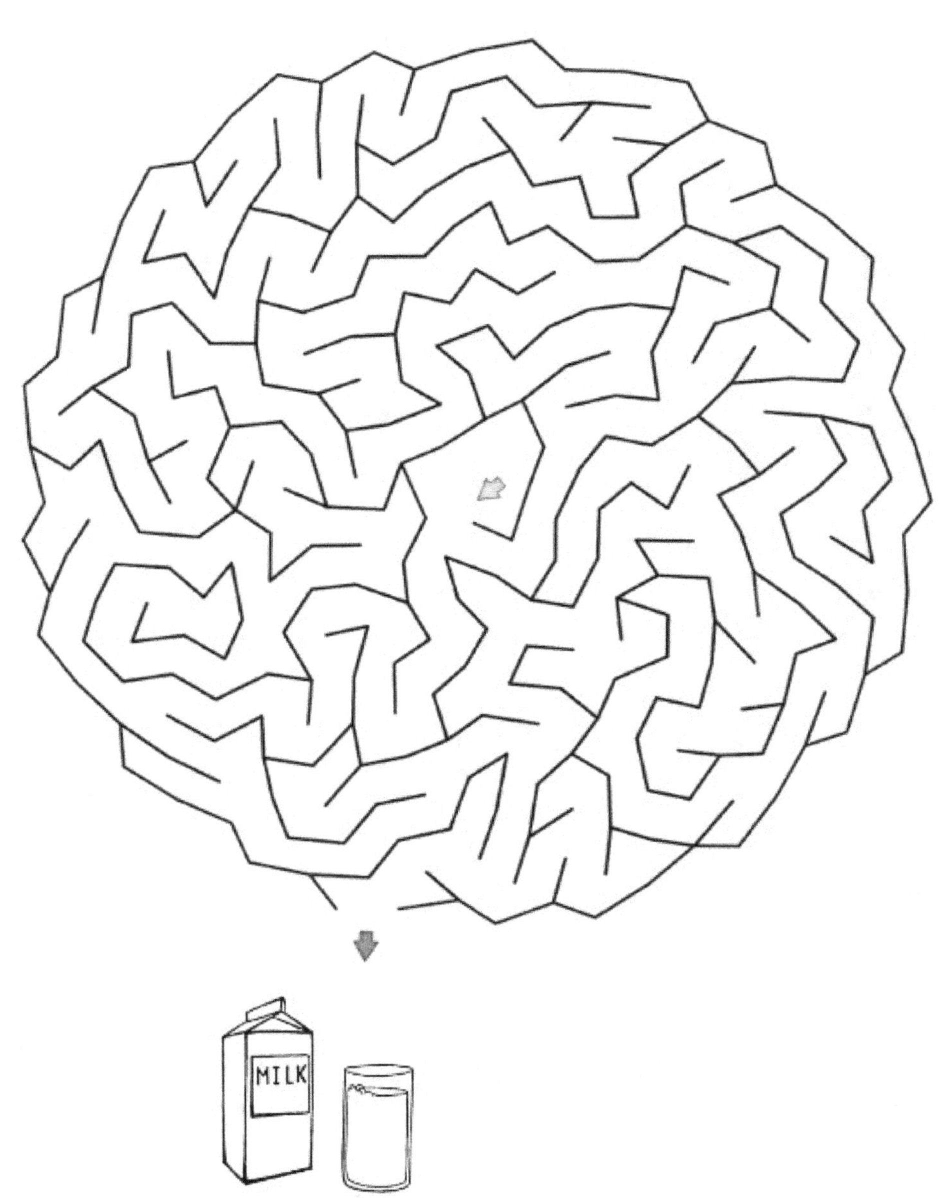
MILK

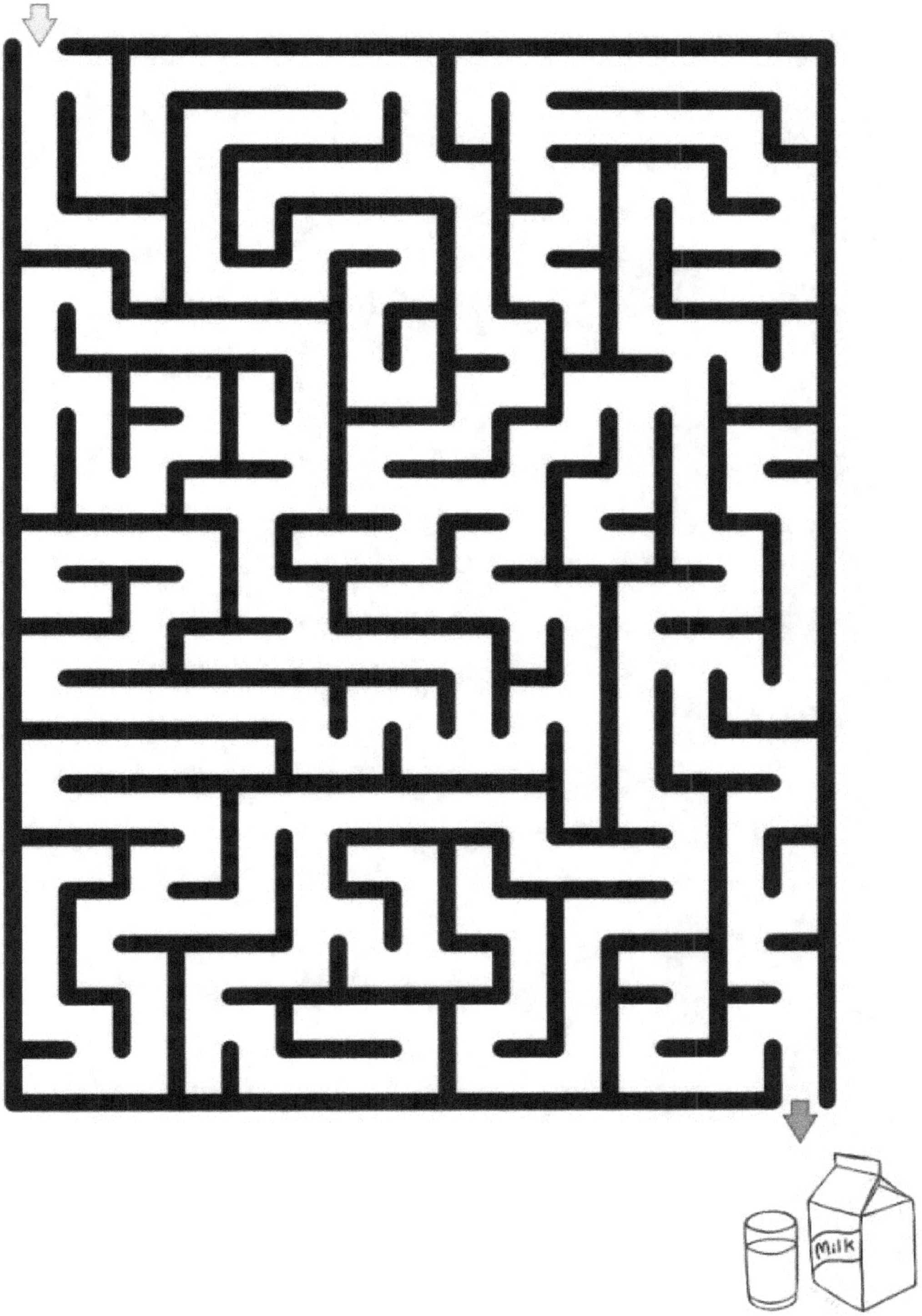

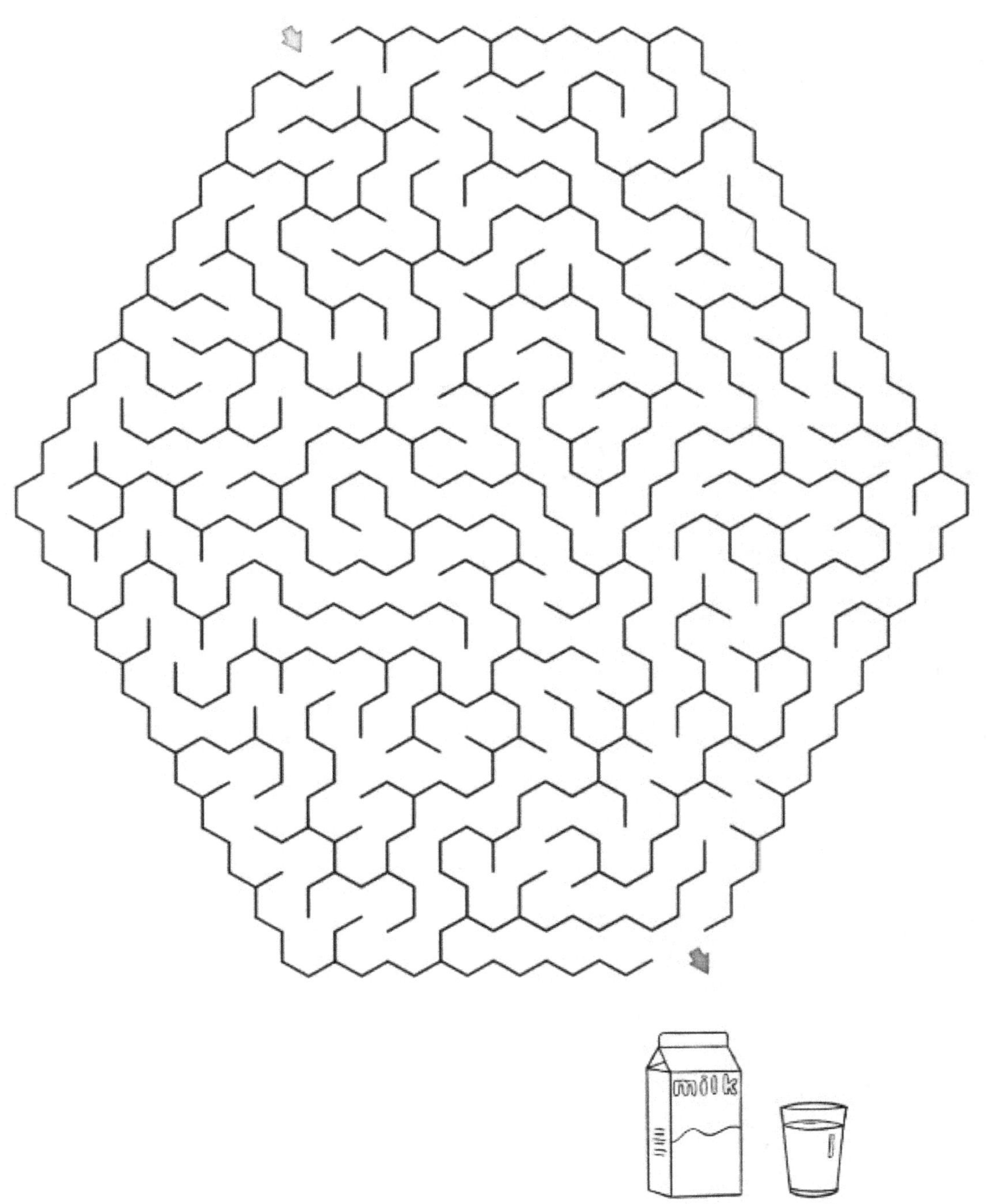
milk

Milk

milk

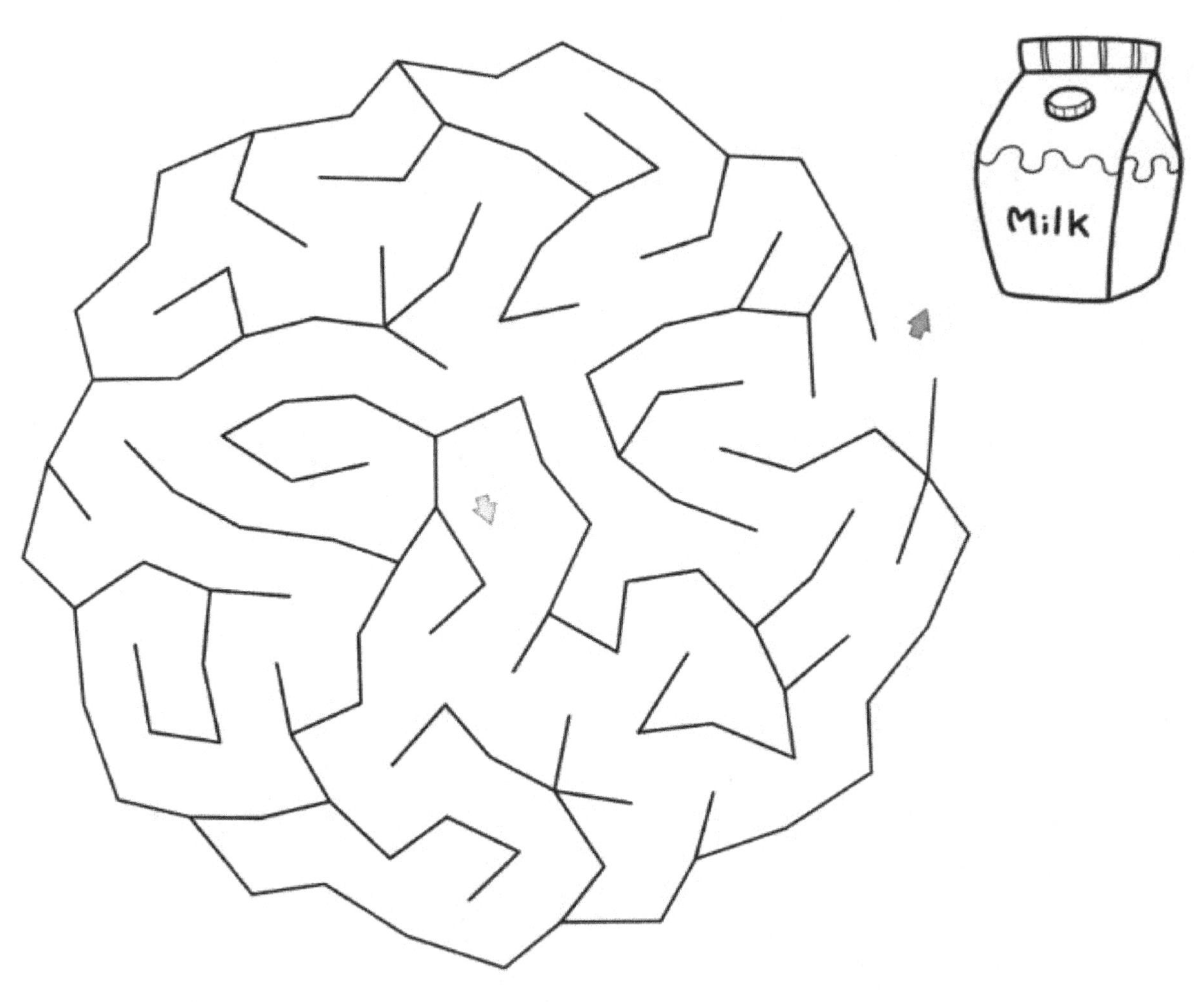
Milk